Stop Pretending You're Being Heard

What to Do When the Message Really Matters

AP Grow

ACKNOWLEDGEMENTS

To my colleagues and clients who shared their thoughts, experiences, and insights to help bring this book to fruition. You're the best! Thank you all.

Table of Contents

DEDICATION

Completing this book would not have been at all possible without the support of my wonderful wife and family. I chose the profession I am in because I needed to make a living and I wanted to make a difference. My wife and family are the motivation and inspiration for both.

.

Introduction

It isn't every day that people are misunderstood. Oh wait, yes it is. As we will get into in the first chapter of this book, misunderstandings can happen for any number of reasons. There is no way we can anticipate every situation that leads to misunderstanding, nor would we want to. What we *can* do is establish and put into practice a set of steps that can improve the chances for successful communication in any situation.

So, you've had a challenge or two communicating with others. I assume this is the case or you wouldn't have a copy of this book in your hands. Don't be too upset at yourself. Countless people face this same challenge every day. My goal with this book is to give you tools and strategies that will help you be more effective in your conversations, whether at work or at home. But before we go any farther, let's be clear about what miscommunications can sometimes look like.

Experiences at Work and at Home

Do either of the following conversations sound familiar?

Hey Mike, how are we coming on the Tarson project?

What do you mean?

The project. Tarson company needs a new PR group. We should present for it. Don't you remember me talking about this last week?

Last week? When?

In the car, on our way to the lunch thing with the Beyo people. Seriously, you don't remember?

No Tom, I don't remember. What makes you so sure you said anything about it. I'm pretty sure I wouldn't be that out to lunch before we even got to lunch.

I did. Mark, this is important. How could you not remember?

Tom, I'm going to stick by my first reaction here. You may have thought about talking about Tarson on our way there but I'm pretty sure I'd remember that. So for now, since it sounds like you have some details on this, why don't you send them to me and I'll start prepping something.

Missing Cues Conversations Take 2

Hey Mike, don't forget we've got the parent social committee this evening.

The what?

Oh no... no. Do NOT tell me you have no clue what I'm talking about?

No, no, it's not like that. Sure I remember we talked about it. But are you sure it's tonight? When did this get on the calendar?

Mike, seriously. YES, I'm sure it's tonight. Two nights ago, just after dinner. Yes, yes, tonight! So you'll be there, right?

I don't know. There's a project Tom dropped on me yesterday. I'll do what I can to get headway on that today to be there tonight.

You better. I'm not going to another one of those things alone.

So what happened here? In both cases what happened? Several things happened actually. Several things happened and several things didn't happen. We'll get into the breakdown of this later. For now, I'd like to suggest that we don't point all fingers at Mike. For now, a different question, the original question asked. Do either of these conversations sound familiar? My guess is they do. Sadly, but not surprisingly, they probably do. Hence this book. In this book I'll present a strategy to improve communication. The goal here is to help not only the Mikes of the world, but more importantly those who are speaking *to* the Mikes of the world.

And in this thought we find the first point of this book – the title, *Stop Pretending You are Being Heard*. The earlier conversations reveal that Mike's workmate and his spouse both *thought* they had been heard. These conversations also demonstrate that such was not the case. The frustrating thing for Mike is both speakers are positive they said what they said they did. And, in both cases, Mike is equally sure things were not said. Who is right is not the point. The point here is that communication faltered. The strategies presented in this book will help correct this and in the process help you be more productive in your communication.

In writing this book I have three purposes in mind,
1) Highlight the fact that effective communication requires more than just saying words, 2) Present a communication model to use as you speak with others, and 3) Provide a tools and strategies that will help you leverage this model to be more effective as you communicate with others.

Chapter 1- How Communication Works

I can't think of an eloquent way to say this so I'll just come out with it. The way most people think communication goes is not the way communication goes. Let's look first at the usual way people think about communication, and then a more realistic view

Most people think that communication goes something like this.

1. Person A speaks
2. Person B hears the message, understands the message as it was intended to be understood, and remembers the message as well.

A diagram of these two steps would look like this.

A ⟶ B

Simple enough, right? Clean, simple, easy to comprehend, easy to follow. The problem is that communication is often not so clean, not so simple, not so straightforward. It would be nice if it were, but it's not, not all the time. The two conversation vignettes shared in the Introduction point out what happens when people assume the straight-line action when in fact what is thought to be happening during a conversation and what is actually happening are two different things.

The concepts I'm about to share here have been presented many ways by many different people. Here is what I think is a decent composite of the many communication models that are out there. First, the diagram again, then, an explanation of the parts, one part at a time.

A ——————————→ B

A – Originator of the Message

With the direct line model, the speaker, A, is the one with the message to share. Let's consider ourselves as this person for the moment. Whether we realize it or not we come to every communication moment with a whole set of presuppositions and predispositions in us. We have our own life experiences, education, biases, family situation, our likes, our dislikes, our cultural heritage, education, work situations and a number of other variables that all factor in to how we think, feel, act, and speak in any given situation. This is where we start.

Too often we run on autopilot with our thoughts, feelings, actions and words. We don't realize how our own experiences feed into the way we present information; the assumptions we make about others, how we assess situations, and the impact all of this has on our words and how we present them. The first step in anyone's path towards more effective communication is to realize that these influences do exist, that they have an impact on us, and that to be most effective in communication we need to control for these elements rather than be controlled by them.

Okay, I'll concede that what I just called 'the first step' is actually a number of steps that are linked together.

The Communication Tunnel

As a child, or perhaps more recently as a team building activity, you've likely participated in an activity usually called The Telephone Activity'. This is the activity where one person starts, whispers into the ear of the one next to them and then around the circle it goes until the person at the end of the line repeats what they think they heard. In your experience, has the originating message *ever* come out the other end the way it started in the beginning? No? It hasn't for me either. I suspect most have had the same experience. The message just doesn't get through.

In the telephone game, as in life, there are a number of reasons why communication may fail. What may seem like a straightforward situation on the surface reveals itself, with a closer inspection, as a much more involved process. Consider the following diagram:

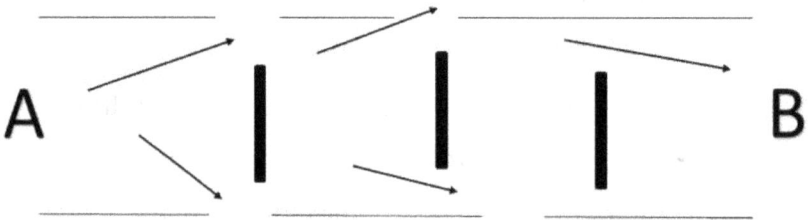

Once again, A is the one sending the message and B is the intended receiver. A has all of the predispositions listed earlier and even more. Before getting distracted with all the walls, holes, gaps, and arrows, in the above figure, let's focus first on the sender of the message.

The State of the Speaker

When we speak we do so from a certain perspective, our own. We say what we think needs said in the way we think it should be said. This is natural. What do we draw on as we choose our words? We say what we think will best meet the needs of the situation based on our experiences, our knowledge, our mood, the sum of our experiences with the one we are speaking to, and an assessment of the situation. All these things and more are used to decide the words we will choose to say and how we will say them. Let's dive deeper into this.

Experiences

When a person is raised in a situation where there is a lot of arguing, contention, or, "spirited negotiation," what do you think their natural form of communication will be like? Can you guess? Of course you can. One doesn't need a psychology degree to know the answer to this. People who grow up in situations where these things are the norm are very likely to communicate this way as *their* norm. Right?

Now consider the opposite environment from what was just discussed; a place where all is pleasant and well. What would you suspect a person from this type of background to be like in their day to day communication? Pleasant? Friendly? Trusting? One would hope so. Whichever situation one has as their background, pleasant, argumentative, or somewhere in between, the chances are pretty good that what they are accustomed to will be their norm as they communicate with others. Now think about yourself. What is your default communication emotion? Is it what you want it to be? If not, be more mindful of it and change.

Education / Knowledge

Have you ever had a college course from an instructor who exuded the feeling that he or she knew everything there was to know on the subject being taught? Most folks who go to college get at least one "Dr. God". When Dr. God speaks, what feelings emote from him or her? Are they happy, comfortable, warm vibes? Probably not. The thing about conceit is it is the only disease that impacts everyone but the one who has it. Speakers who project conceit are not likely to have people around ready to listen. A tad ironic when the attitudes that shuts others down is coming from a supposed teacher, but we'll set that aside for now. The important point here is that the attitude we project, whatever the source of that attitude, can also impact *how* we communicate. Those who think they know everything will state their messages a certain way. They will say certain things, and say these things in certain ways and these things together will have an impact on how the messages are received.

The Dr. God illustration may be an extreme case but it illustrates the point well I think. There are know-it-all types who, by their very nature, turn people off as they speak (and in the process create a barrier to being heard or heeded). Another case that falls into this category are situations when the speaker has knowledge that he or she believes others also know. Assumptions are made and, in the process, miscommunications happen. Here is a common example that will illustrate this; a call between two coworkers.

Tom, where are you? We have a meeting with the client now.

I was going to ask you the same question. You said be here at 9:00. I'm here!

Where? Because I'm here too and I don't see you; the Spearman offices, 9:00.

The Spearman offices? I'm at the Forresters!

Miscommunications like this happen every day. When we have knowledge we make certain assumptions. This can cause us to leave out details that we assume the other person knows. We all know the phrase that connects with the dangers of making assumptions. What's the fix? Share the information – all of it. Why risk the miscommunication? Make no assumptions about what someone else knows. Whatever details there are to share, you share them.

Setting

If your boss has something he or she wants to share, what are these different surroundings going to suggest? Let's play a quick matching game.

Topic	Probable Setting
The upcoming office picnic	In the break room
Conversation about upcoming movies	In the boss's office
Addressing bad performance at work	At the bus stop outside the office

Granted, each one of the topics listed could happen in any of the settings also listed. However, I think (I hope) most would agree that the conversation about addressing bad performance should happen in the office. The other two are perhaps interchangeable.

Pop quiz. If you need to tell an employee that they need to do better about getting to work on time, which of the above settings would you choose? I sincerely hope you'd go with 'boss's office'. Try giving important information to a subordinate while laughing it up in the company breakroom and see how far that gets you. Can you imagine how that would go?

"Oh my goodness Tom, that was hilarious. Oh by the way, I need you to start getting to work on time or there will be problems, okay? Great!"

Does something seem a bit disjointed here? It *should* seem disjointed, because it *is* disjointed. An important message said in an informal situation and in an informal, 'no big deal' way is problematic. The above scenario is likely to leave Tom wondering if you really mean what you are saying. You don't want Tom wondering.

The point is this; setting can impact expectations about what the message is supposed to be. Setting can also impact how messages are received. Different settings can suggest different things. The more formal the environment, the more important the matter. At least that's how it should be. There is a reason a person will (or should) choose a nice location to propose marriage. There is a reason the boss suggests the office for a serious chat. We'll pick up on this again later in the book.

Attitude about the Listener

The way people might adjust their speaking based on who they are speaking with is a fluid element. Sometimes changes in approach based on who one is speaking to is an intended change, as in times when speaking to a child (or someone who is acting like a child). Other times, changes based on attitude about a listener are not intended. If two people have a history, for example, this history can impact how a speaker speaks, as well as how a listener listens. One should be able to easily see how this can impact communication. Imagine if two people were romantically involved in the past. If the relationship ended amicably, then interaction should be comfortable, right? If the relationship ended poorly, well, we all know how well communication between two divorced people can go. You get the picture.

The State of the 'Listener'

The reason 'listener' is being put in quotation marks here is because we assume that the one we are speaking to is actually listening. But this is not always the case. In fact, this is often not the case. Hence the name of this book and the reason for it - Stop Pretending You're being Heard. If the one we are speaking to isn't really hearing us, then it's our pretending that keeps the 'conversation' going. Better to make our conversations genuine rather than pretend. That's my thinking anyway.

This is really the other side of the conversation. We addressed the speaker's side of things, now it's time to consider the listener's side. Like the speaker, the listener also comes to any communication moment with a collection of thoughts in mind. Knowledge, feelings about a situation, and even feelings about the person speaking all contribute to how a listener 'hears' what someone is saying to them.

Think about it. Who would you be more likely to pay attention to, someone you know and respect, or someone you don't know or don't particularly respect? We are human. In most cases we can't help but feel how we feel. It is these feelings that can impact how we take in information.

Prior Knowledge

Have you ever had a friend try to tell you about a sports game they watched on TV that you had attended in person? You listened, or rather pretended to listen for a while. You were polite, smiling. And then, at the time you thought it might be most entertaining, you told your reporter friend you were actually at the game so no need to hear the TV-based report. Your friend says something sarcastic and then moves on to something else. Question: While your friend was telling you about the game, were you listening? Of course you weren't. You were thinking about the weather, putting gas in your car, maybe your hot date later that day… your mind was on anything but the words of your friend. Why? Because you were *there*. What more can you learn about it from someone who watched it on TV?

Feeling like you've just been busted? Don't. At work and in life, this is what many people do. People who know, or think they know what's being said, typically don't listen. We'll respond with appropriate 'response sounds' to make it seem like we're listening, but we're not. Not really. Adults are usually pretty good at making it *look* like they are listening. Teenagers, not so much. Right? So here's the thing to keep in mind. If there is any question, assume the person you are speaking to has already heard what you are saying. With this thought in mind, what adjustments would you make? Think on that question for a bit. I'll share some thoughts on this in the next chapter.

Disposition

Disposition has a connection to background knowledge. A person who thinks they know what's being said may not listen carefully. A person who knows they don't know anything about what's being said is likely to pay at least a little more attention. Similarly, if a listener is 'in the moment' they'll be with you and focus on what you are saying. If their heart, mind, or thoughts are somewhere else, perhaps bothered by something that happened earlier in the day, or concerned with something else going on in their world - stressed, worried, or perhaps angry - chances are their thoughts won't be focused on you and your words.

Distractions

Have you ever had the pleasure of trying to speak to someone while they are watching a sporting event? How did that go? We all know what the answer is. It probably didn't go well. Try talking to a fashion fan, when a fashion show is on. You will likely have the same experience – not a particularly 'in tune' one. In the workplace, the situation is not much different. The source of the distraction will be different - an outlandish email, a frustrated client, an overbearing boss - but the result will be the same.

Physical Noise

Not to fall into any particular pattern (though I'm doing it anyway) I'll start this section with another question. Have you ever had the pleasure of attempting a conversation in a busy subway tunnel? How did *that* work out for you? Not an easy task, right? Construction site, seated in a crowd at a sports event, busy cafe at midday - these are a few more examples of noisy places where people try to communicate. Personally, I always wondered how folks who work on the floors of the stock exchange ever get anything done. The point is this, noise, actual, physical noise, can also hinder effective communication.

As with any recovery program, recognition is the first step. This chapter pointed out multiple examples of what you need to recognize as you prepare for conversations. What you say and how you say it should be determined based on all the variables you can identify.

Chapter 2 – Minimizing the 'Noise'

In Chapter 1 I shared with you my definition of noise, that which interferes with communication. You learned there are a lot of types of noise. It was stated earlier, though I'll repeat here for good measure, that there is no way to identify all of the different types of noise one might encounter when communicating with others. Still, we'll go through a few of the noise categories to give you an idea of what can be done to take care of this first step in improving communication.

Actual physical noise is one type of noise, a barrier to communication. Typically this isn't an issue with office environments but it can be a problem on construction sites and on the streets. For office situations, the types of noise that more often impedes communication include biases, preconceptions, misconceptions, the emotional or mental state of the speaker, the mental or emotional state of the listener; so many possibilities. In this chapter we are going to get into many of the most common barriers and look at ways to lessen their impact on effective communication.

Age

There is so much information about how age all by itself can create barriers in communication. Whole books, seminars, and training organizations have been created to address the differences in communication connected with age and generational differences. Labels to categorize whole age groups are readily recognized, Generation X, Generation Y, and Millennials are abels given to certain age groups. Connected with all these names is a set of researched, quazi-researched, and inferred characteristics that are often cited, and many times mis-cited too. Our present era is not the first to have people say of the younger generation, "They just don't get it."

If age might be a cause for noise between you and someone you are speaking with, the best recommendation I can offer is to put yourself in the place of the one you are speaking with. As best as you can, determine what their own situation is, where they've been in life, where they may be going, and how the present moment might fit into their reality. Of course there's no way to know any of this unless you happen to be a mind reader or know the person that well, so the action to take is to be conversational. Ask the questions that make sense to ask to get to know the other person better. This will be the smart strategy whether the person you are speaking with is older or younger. Don't assume anything. Sure, we all have different backgrounds to some degree. Age is just one of those things that can heighten challenges where ordinary differences may already exist. Rather than fight it, work with it. Recognize it is there. Look for ways to minimize the barricades that it can bring.

This is particularly true with interactions between parents and children. Having been a parent of teenagers myself, I can attest to the challenges that age differences can sometimes bring. What I think is most interesting is how they will sometimes discuss ideas that I have never thought of. It's clear to me that there are influences beside my own that impact their thinking. Fighting this reality is futile. So the best course of action I can think of is to try to understand the differences through communication. With a better understanding between parent and child one can approach whatever has to be said in a way that might be best received when the message is delivered.

Parent-child communication is a field unto itself. Countless books have been written on this topic so I don't see a need to dive into it too deeply here. Suffice it to say that it is definitely an area where even experts struggle. So if you're struggling with communication between yourself and children don't feel bad, you're not alone. Most times, in most situations, children grow up and all families can communicate like regular human beings.

Education / Background Knowledge

Education can be a barrier to communication, particularly if the one with more education holds this up as a thing. Some of the smartest people I know stopped their formal education after high school. Conversely, some of the biggest idiots I have ever come across hold doctoral degrees. Formal education does not have to be a barrier to communication, but it can be. It can be a barrier to communication when there are assumptions about what somebody knows or doesn't know.

Consider this example. Have you ever been in a class where the subject being taught is the teacher's most favorite subject? I've had the pleasure of this experience on a few occasions. Here I am using the phrase "pleasure" in a sarcastic way because I've had similar experiences. The teacher will begin speaking and almost immediately it's as if the professor was speaking a different language. Actually, in a way, a professor who is teaching in their area of specialization kind of is speaking a different language, regardless of the subject matter.

It's been said that knowing a subject is only a matter of knowing the words of that subject. So if I don't happen to know the intricacies of the Torricelli's law and the teacher started her lecture with this concept, she may as well be speaking Greek. But I digress, back to the point. Teachers can sometimes fail in communicating with students when they jump ahead in their subject matter because they make certain assumptions that the students in their class already know the more basic elements of the topic being discussed. They do this because they know the subject so well that it is second nature to them; as if everybody around them also knows the information as well as they do The problem is that everyone does *not* know everything about the subject being taught. To assume so, and to continue speaking as if this were the case, leaves others in the dust.

But educational settings are not the only place where this can occur. Anytime a manager or another supervisor has had additional training or experience in a given area, there is the danger of assuming that others around them have this same knowledge. Many times they will start down a road conversationally and, if background understanding isn't checked first, those they are speaking to also get lost.

Whether it's home or work related let's get to some solutions for reducing knowledge-related, "noise." For starters, it's important to make absolutely no assumptions. Do not assume that because you know about a subject the person you're speaking with also knows the subject. Sometimes we know this *isn't* the case. When this *is* the case, some people like to play on this by saying, "I have a secret" said in a singsong way.

Playing like this is fine for a time, but if we're not sure whether the other person has the needed background information for the conversation we're about to have the best strategy is to find out if this is actually the case or not. How do we do this? Let me first tell you how not to do this. Avoid questions such as, "Do you know about X?" This is an example of what is typically called a closed question. It requires nothing more than a simple yes or no as a reply. If the person you are speaking to says, "No," then there is not likely to be any noise caused by this lack of background knowledge, because you know the score and you'll fill in the gaps.

The more perilous situation is when the person you are speaking to says, "Yes." The potential hazard here is two-fold, 1) They think they know about the subject, when in fact they don't. Or, 2) they know only a little bit about the subject, and that little bit does not include the background knowledge that is necessary to a better understand the message you want to share. With incorrect assumptions it may not be until you are further into the dialogue that you realize the background knowledge isn't what it needed to be, with a good deal of productivity lost in the process – another form of noise.

The best strategy for reducing this type of noise is to start by providing the necessary background information. If the one you're speaking to has this knowledge, they will say so. Then you can move forward with a greater certainty that the two of you are on the same page. If they don't have the needed background information then you provide it, and move forward from there.

Here's a brief dialogue between George and Biff to illustrate a noise-reducing strategy that has to do with education and knowledge background. George starts the conversation.

Are you up on the Stanison project?

Sure, I know all about them.

Great, then tell me why they are deciding to go with a different company for their marketing.

Wait, what?

This misunderstanding of what George was expecting Biff to know was quickly discovered because George got right to the missing piece in his second question. Not uncommonly, the person who asks if they are up to speed on something simply hears the "yes" and then they keep talking - as if they know the other person's knowledge is sufficient to handle what they're about to share. Only later is it realized that the other person did not, in fact, know everything they needed to know to have an effective conversation. So, again, the best strategy for reducing noise related to background knowledge is to share all background knowledge that may be needed for your listener to understand. Don't assume, overshare.

Cultural

Culture is kind of a loaded word. Not kind of, it is. Many people come across somebody from a different cultural background and immediately think there is going to be a challenging communication. Sometimes this is true, but certainly not always. It is not a given that there is going to be, "noise" with respect to culture.

I've added this category here because in many ways it is not unlike barriers that can get in the way because of education or background knowledge. A person's culture is the sum of their life experiences. The food they eat, their values, thoughts about others, animals, politics, family, work, and many other topics can all be tied to one's culture. This holds true whether we're speaking of culture in the more general sense as what is represented by different countries and with different races, or in a more specific sense as in one's own family situation, or the neighborhood they grew up in. All of this touches on the insights, knowledge, and feelings about how one sees the world and how they interpret information that they receive.

Minimizing noise due to cultural differences between people is best done by focusing on what is in fact similar between the people who are involved in the conversations. Those things that people around the world have in common I like to refer to as human universals.

Human universals, as the phrase implies, are elements of life that all people have in common. For example, the notion of beauty exists around the world. True what may be seen as beautiful will vary from person-to-person and from culture to culture but the concept exists everywhere. Similarly, life is valued in all cultures. Again, how this value is demonstrated may vary but the notion that life has value is universal.

Family is another concept that crosses all cultural borders. Communicating in terms of parents, children, grandparents, nieces and nephews, will usually cut through complications that can arise through barriers that might otherwise be caused by cultural differences. Here is a personal experience to illustrate the point. As I think on this, I can also say that it touches not only on working across cultural barriers, but across language barriers as well.

Several years ago I was working for a program that hosted international groups to come to the United States to learn English and business related topics. I had turned the management of one of these programs over to a colleague. I thought all was going smoothly until the leader of that client group, a gentleman from Japan arrived in my office one day unannounced. It turns out he was visiting the US for a number of reasons and he made one of his stops my office while he was in the area.

His English language skills were not good. Sadly, my Japanese language skills were even worse so there were some challenges to overcome, I was a bit surprised about this because the exchanges we had had up to this point were quite fluent. I realized at that moment that he had been using an assistant to write his exchanges with me. So there we were, him without his assistant and me not able to speak in his native language. This was before the days of readily available web-based and mobile-based translation programs. Nevertheless, he overcame this challenge and in the process taught me the value of considering others in terms of human universals.

While we were trying to converse, he looked at a picture of me with my family that I had in my office. He pointed to the picture and said simply, "Your family?" I smiled, nodded, and said only one word, "Yes." He then said, "You talk to them?"

I was a bit surprised by the question but gave a similar reply, "Yes." Then it was his turn to smile as he said simply, "I need more of that."

The lightbulb went on. I thought my colleague had been doing a fine job of communicating with the group leader in preparations for the group that was to be coming in a few months. And maybe in the opinion of my colleague this was the case. But, according to my client, the one I was hoping to foster a very long-term connection with, this wasn't the case. He made it clear in just a few words that there was something we needed to attend to and I was very grateful that he did.

I share this experience with respect to culture and the noise that can get in the way of communication due to cultural differences because, in the view of my subordinate, everything was fine, but to our client, all was not well. Yes, one may say this could have been personal-based differences as well. Perhaps. There's not a big need to pin down the exact breakdown, our goal is to be sure to have tools to overcome them, as my client from Japan did. My client friend was astute enough to see how family is a human universal and what I did with my family was probably exactly what he did with his family and through that, he bridged our communication gap.

Clearly, this example would work equally well in overcoming language barriers. But I wanted to stress the human universal element here which is why I put the example in this section. Now let's look at communication barriers that can rise from language differences.

Language Barriers

We live in a wonderful time; a time when transportation, changing demographics, and technological advances affords us opportunities to interact with people from around the world. When it comes to interacting with others who speak English as their second language, what used to be an uncommon occurrence in many parts of the US is now a very regular thing. Yet there are many who are not comfortable with this. In many parts of the world, multilingual abilities, and being comfortable with cross-language situations are common and has been for centuries. In the US, this has not been the case.

Times are different now. For this reason it is in the best interest of anyone who wants to become most effective in leadership situations to be comfortable in cross-language communication. As I have been involved in the international scene throughout most of my career, I could talk for hours about this topic. When I mention working with those whose English language skills are not so strong, I am often asked,

"How do you do it?"

There are several strategies for overcoming language barriers. Here I will share just a few that can help reduce the blocks that can come up due to language. For starters, consider speaking at a slower pace. If you're a person who is often told even by friends or family to slow down as you speak, this piece of advice is for you. If you are a fast talker, chances of miscommunication become even higher when trying to communicate with somebody whose first language is not English. So, tip number one, slow down.

Suggestion two, when there are misunderstandings, do not say the same words or phrases over and over again, or worse, repeat the same words or phrases BUT IN A LOUDER VOICE! Instead, consider using synonymous phrases; ways to convey the same meaning with different words. This has a much better chance of helping you get understood.

Idea number three; technology in our time makes it extremely easy to use mobile-based applications to overcome language barriers. Translation services readily available through the Internet or as apps on smart phones make it easy to obtain immediate and accurate language translations. With these tools in hand, it's amazing how much one can communicate across language barriers. I am not above using these technologies to convey accurate messages across language barriers. You shouldn't be either.

Physical Setting

Physical setting can make or break a lot of different communication situations. There is a reason a suitor will take an intended spouse to a nice restaurant or other romantic location to propose marriage. A nice location is a most appropriate setting for such an important question. There is a reason a boss will invite a subordinate to his or her office to have that "coming to Jesus" conversation regarding, for example, the need to stop gossiping in the office. Settings suggest something. This was discussed in the previous chapter when the topic of noise was introduced. This chapter is about reducing this type of noise.

If you need to speak to a subordinate about their work performance, you do this in your office; not the break room, not the hallway, not outside at the bus stop while you both happen to be there waiting to get on the bus. This is so basic I don't see a need to go any further about this except to close with this; do whatever needs to be done to match setting with message. If these two items are out of sync, your message is likely to be not nearly as effective as it could be.

On a related topic, sometimes we discount the impact of

being in a noisy environment. Here I mean actual, very audible noise. Hectic offices, busy street corners, loud cars, loud homes - these are all instances where actual physical noise can get in the way of communication. The fix, of course, is relatively simple; find quieter places to be, or, if possible, reduce the noise where you are. Turn down the TV or radio. Ask other people to leave the room, or move to another room yourself. Ask children to quiet down or fall asleep. Put the dogs outside; whatever it takes to get a quieter environment for your conversation, that's what you do. Making the effort to create the best setting for the message you mean to share will always be worth the time.

On the topic of setting, here's a related matter. Sometimes, we cannot choose our conversation settings. Sometimes situations choose us. As an example, when your boss steps into the elevator and asks you how a certain project is coming along. If you're not ready to respond to that question what do you do? Wouldn't it be great if you could reply, "You know boss I'm not fully prepared to answer you on that topic right this second, why don't you stop by my office later this afternoon and we can chat about it."

I'm not sure that would be a good idea. Actually, I'm pretty sure that would *not* be a good idea. Some of the best advice I ever received as a young employee was this. Don't wait to be asked about the status of a project before thinking on it.

When you stop work for a time on any project you are working on, ask yourself, "If somebody were to ask me the status of this right now, what would I say?" That advice has come in handy too many times to count. So I share this with you now in the hope that it will do you the same amount of good. We cannot always choose our setting, but we can choose to be ready to deliver our message in a clear, concise manner when the need arises. This can be especially valuable if the message is important or the person we're speaking to is a higher up, and the time is limited.

Emotional State

Let me ask you a question. When you're upset how well do you think you listen?

I'll tell you what research has to say on this topic. The answer is, not well. Being upset, whatever the cause, creates within individuals a myriad of internal distractions which drastically reduces one's ability to focus on a message that someone else is attempting to send. Please don't make the mistake of thinking that you are any different than the average human with respect to this phenomena. You're not, and neither is the person you might want to talk to. If they are upset, regardless of the cause, if the message you want to share does not relate to what they are upset about, chances are your message will not be heard, .

Most people don't question this with respect to domestic conversations. A countless number of books have already been written on this topic. If a spouse is upset, it is best to wait until time has passed before having a desired conversation. The evidence is clear. Both individual experience and academic research demonstrates; quality communication simply does not happen when people are in distressed emotional states.

The fix? Wait until this unproductive emotional state has passed. If your observation of the situation suggests it is not the best time to communicate, if the message can wait, then let it wait. Set up a new time. Until that next time, do what needs done to give yourself the best chance of saying what needs to be said - when the one you want to speak with is in the best state to receive your message.

I will concede, sometimes this is easier said than done. Sometimes a message cannot wait; whatever needs to be said has to be said regardless of the emotional state the other person is in. When this happens, do your best to make the message short; concise. Say what needs to be said and leave. Leave the individual to deal with whatever it is they are dealing with. Follow up later to determine if the brief message you leave with them has gotten processed.

Mental State

When it comes to working with others, be it for success on a team or considering how best to communicate with family, friends, or somebody else, many sources discuss mental and emotional state in the same category. This is understandable. Certainly one's emotional state can impact their mental state. And there's a good amount of research that suggests one's mental state can in fact influence an emotional state. The mind can in fact control the body, or rather how a body feels.

I'm calling mental state out as a different category because of how I am defining it. I could have just as easily called this category, Focus. If the one you want to communicate with has their focus on something else, don't expect to have a very productive exchange with them. End of story, mic drop, done. It's that simple. If they are watching something on TV, for example, you're kidding yourself if you think they are actually listening when they say, "Go ahead, I'm listening." They may *think* they're listening, but they're not. It is this scenario, this exact situation, I had in mind when I came up the title, Stop Pretending You're Being Heard. If you think you're being heard in these situations, you'd better think again.

To be fair, the person who says, "Go ahead, I'm listening,"

might actually be working to hear the words you have to say. The problem is, they are doing this at the same time they are trying to listen to the words or watch the action on the TV in front of them, or listening to a song on the radio, or a conversation happening next to you, or contemplating their next move on a video game. The mind is an impressive organ, but for all its power, it cannot process two items at the same time. Hence, in these situations, attention will suffer. My recommendation, don't fight it. Instead, recognize it, and wait until it is clear you have their focus. Later in the book we'll cover strategies for how to do this.

Related to this are situations where you *think* you have the attention of the one you are speaking to and so you share whatever it is you want to share. Why do you think you have their attention? Because you decided you wanted to share something so of course it must be an okay time to share, right? I say this only half in gest.

We are human. And being human we tend to want to do whatever it is we want to do whenever we want to do it. If, for example, we think that it is a fine time to share a piece of information, then by golly it is a fine time to share the information. Never mind what the other person might have going on in his or her mind. We share what we wish to share when we wish to share it, and damn the consequences. But therein lies the problem. It's not what we want that matters.

It's whether or not the person we are speaking to is actually paying attention. And just because you decide it's time to say something is no reason to expect the other person is ready to hear it. This is not so much a barrier to listening as it is a matter of preparing the listener. For this reason we will take up this particular topic in the next chapter. For now, just be aware that your desire to be heard doesn't automatically mean the other person is ready to listen.

Past Experiences

Pop quiz. Who would you most prefer to listen to; somebody you know and respect, or somebody you don't know, or worse, you know them and you don't respect them? If you are like most people you're going to go with option A. You will prefer to listen to somebody you know and respect. This is human nature. And, because it is human nature, it is an important element to keep in mind when you are working with other people. What do they think about you? Are you approaching somebody that you've never met before to ask them for help? If so, you may want to start with at least a little bit of small talk before you ask for the favor.

In the communication training that I provide for organizations this is one of the most common pieces of advice I give. If you walk past the same person or the same office every day (who doesn't) and you have never said hello to that person or the people in that office, it's time to change. It's time to change not only for the human element of recognizing that everyone is worth saying hello to, it's time to change for the more practical reason that the chances are pretty good at some point you're going to need help from those individuals. Yes, I said it, I'm speaking of selfish reasons for being more conversational with others. Though it should be noted that being friendly to others is its own reward.

If you have been a kind, pleasant, smile-inducing type of person with others, you will have greatly increased your chances that you will get the help you need when you need it; even if the request is somewhat urgent and puts them out of their own work cycle. Try making an urgent request of somebody that doesn't know you; particularly if you had about a thousand chances to get to know them earlier. You get the picture – past experience matters. Don't let this element ever be a barrier to communication. Take every opportunity to be friendly with everyone. Be pleasant, be considerate, and be helpful. This way, when the time comes that you need assistance or you have a message that needs to be conveyed even if it isn't all that pleasant to share, at least this one element will not be a barrier to the task.

In this chapter we've gone over several elements that can impede communication. You've gotten several ideas about how to overcome noise so that the natural barriers that might come up as you speak with others can be reduced or eliminated. These are the first questions to consider when speaking with others; what barriers might there be, and how can I work to reduce them? Asking these two questions before entering into conversations where information needs to be shared and remembered will help increase the chances of your success as you move into the next steps of the process. I get how formulaic all of this seems - to take something so natural as communication and turn it into a step-by-step process. But I can promise you that as you think about these things more intentionally, you will find more success as you interact with others.

The next step in the 'get heard' process is insuring others are truly ready to hear what we have to say. This is what Chapter 3 is all about.

Chapter 3 - Preparing the Listener

In my youth I attended summer camp. Every year at summer camp one of the activities that I enjoyed the most was the rifle range. Of course I was not alone in this. Many kids like to get on the firing line to shoot several rounds into a target. Heck, even many adults like doing this. My reason for enjoying this, however, was perhaps a bit different then for others. I was raised in Oregon's Willamette Valley, wine country of the Pacific Northwest. Shooting rifles was not new to me. My first experiences with small caliber rifles was long before I ever got to summer camp. I enjoyed the rifle range at summer camp because it was my opportunity to show off.

Yes, here for the first time, I am going to admit that I have a bit of an issue with pride. My accuracy with a 22 rifle with the target at 50 feet was pretty good. As a kid I did not have the money to go to sporting goods store and pick up a package of paper targets. The best I could do was put smaller and smaller objects on a sawhorse and see if I could hit them from 50 feet. Back then, pop cans, then smaller tin cans, then pill bottles were my targets. As the summers stacked up, I begin propping up quarters, nickels, and dimes to see if I could also hit these at 50 feet. The quarters usually got hit; the nickels and dimes, not as often. The point is this; hitting these objects took practice. It didn't happen automatically and it was certainly never would have happened if I hadn't set things up right and practiced.

I think this is a pretty decent analogy for when we have a message that we want to share. They have to be prepared and if they're not prepared chances of hitting your mark are pretty slim. At summer camp, I would watch as the guys on either side of me at the rifle range would prepare their target. There were wires running from left to right at the end of the firing range, and every one would use clothes pins to hold their target to these wires at the top and bottom of the target.

Sometimes I would see targets that were pinned in a way that created a bend in the paper target. Those who did this made it virtually impossible for themselves to get a good result - even if they happened to be fairly good at shooting. Others wouldn't bother pinning the bottom of the target to the bottom wire which may have seemed okay as they were doing it but if by chance the wind picked up after everyone got back to the firing line their target would twist in the wind and, again, make it essentially impossible to hit the target. If there isn't adequate preparation of the target, even the best delivery might be useless. So let's talk now about preparing targets, in this case the intended receiver of your communication.

How do the following words strike you?

"We need to talk."

I suspect I am not the only person in the world who, upon hearing these words, gets a tad nervous. Why is this? I can't answer for everyone, but in my life, these words typically mean there is something important that needs to be said and sometimes the important topic is not one that I am all that comfortable discussing. This, however, does not mean that the topic doesn't need to be discussed. My wanting to avoid a topic does not take away the importance of the topic. My good wife knows this and so when there are instances that I must stop everything that I'm doing, clear all thoughts from my head, and focus 100% on what she has to say, these are the words she will use. It has become her surefire way to prepare me, the intended recipient, of her message.

Now, I will say that these words are often followed by another phrase which is also very helpful. "It doesn't have to be right now, but at some point in the next day or two we need to talk about...." I like this approach because it does two things. First, it tells me that there is something that is important to her and if for no other reason than this it needs to be important to me too. Second, at the same time, saying these words also conveys a recognition that I can't typically stop everything that I have going on in my schedule or in my head with little or no notice and focus 100% on what she needs to share. I appreciate this consideration. I appreciate it a lot. But I don't think my appreciation is what matters most to her in these situations. It's probably more the fact that when the time comes, I will be ready to listen.

The question for you of course is what do you need to do to prepare your listener? In this chapter I'm going to give you several strategies for preparing your listener. Most of the strategies are going to be interchangeable, meaning they can work equally well in home situations, in work situations, or in community/social situations. Your job will be to take all of these possible strategies and tools, consider them, and combine them as needed, for the best possible result based on the situation and the individual(s) you are planning to speak to. To this end, I believe there are three factors that have to be considered, the person or people, the time and place, and the message. Let's look at each of these individually.

Preparing the Message

Have you ever attended a conference session or other large meeting and when the main speaker gets up to start, the first words out of their mouth are "I'm really excited to be here but I've got to tell you I don't know exactly what I'm going to say." When you hear these words, or something like them, what is your reaction? I can tell you what mine is. The moment I hear words like these I want to get up and walk out. If a person standing in front of a large group hasn't put in enough time to know what they will say when they are supposed to have the attention of everybody in the room, why on earth should I sit there and listen to it; whatever the "it" is?

As a professional speaker I cannot fathom why somebody would get up in front of others and say anything close to 'I'm not sure what I'm going to say". It absolutely boggles my mind that a speaker would think this is somehow endearing. If I had to guess, I suppose they think this will help garner some sympathy if things don't go well. To anybody who thinks this is a good idea, I would suggest a different way of thinking; a different way of being. Prepare your message so that when you are in front of people, you know exactly what you're going to say. Sure, you may vary your message depending on a developing situation or how listeners react, but the core points that you intend to share before you stand up in front of people should be well in hand. To stand up in front of a number of people and "wing it" is not cute, it is not funny, it is not professional. Don't do it.

Fortunately, most people who are given a task that requires standing in front of others to deliver a message are so scared of this that they will prepare long in advance of the moment. They will, in fact, go to the opposite extreme, writing down every word, and then, in front of the group, only read what they have written - an activity that could have just as easily been done by email and saved everybody a bunch of time. Still, I respect that they are considerate enough of others to have prepared their message and even though some work could be done on the delivery, the fact is they prepared their message and got the job done.

Now here's the scoop of the day. This preparation principle is no less important for you delivering your message to one person as it is to the individual expecting to speak in front of many. This is true regardless of where you are - in the office, at home, or volunteering in a community service group. You should feel no less obligated to prepare what it is you mean to say in front of a small audience, even an audience of one, than you would for a larger group.

Typically, however, this is not what happens. When planning to talk to a single individual, most folks have a general idea of what they want to say and when the moment comes, they stumble through it. Sometimes it works, sometimes it doesn't. Why go into a situation, any situation, where you don't have a very good idea of what you want to say and how you're going to say it? All too often people will treat one-on-one conversations too casually. To be sure, there are times when casual conversation is fine. We have nothing particular we need to say. I'm not talking about those times. I'm talking about times when the message is important, when having the message heard, understood, and remembered is important. In these instances it makes absolutely no sense to walk into the situation with the idea of just "winging it".

Here is a process you can use to help you create the message that you intend to give. First, identify the key points you want to share. I recommend that you keep your message down to no more than three points. Years ago, a psychology professor taught the class that, in general, people can remember up to seven items in a list give or take two. In other words 5 to 9 items. I think that larger number is optimistic. Or what may have been true at one time probably isn't true any longer. Either way why risk it? Most important messages can be whittled down to only a few items. Identify what these items are and you'll have the first step handled.

Second, identify the most concise way of stating these items.

Take some time with this. It's important. Those who make their living off of sharing words know the value of word conservation. Comedians, for example, understand that the economy of language can make or break a joke. I've heard some comedians say they will spend weeks thinking how they can change a one-liner of 10 words to a one-liner of seven words. George Burns put it this way, "Seven is a funny number, ten, not so much. People seem to lose focus after nine or ten. So I like to go with seven." Coming from one who made his living by speaking in front of others, this is probably a message worth remembering.

I know you're not likely to need somebody's attention to tell them a joke. And if this *is* the case, then the importance of getting it right is not so important as if you were, for example, giving directions to save a person's life. Still, the point remains, if you have something important that needs to be said, say it in the most economical way possible. Your chances of having the message remembered will go up to the degree you are able to apply this second step well.

The third step in preparing your message is to decide in what order you want to deliver your ideas. This can be done in a number of different ways. Sometimes a speaker will let the listener decide. They will ask, for example, "Which do you want first, the good news or the bad news?" For most occasions, I would recommend that you decide the presentation order on your own. A traditional pattern is to deliver the less critical information first, and then work up to the most important messages. This has some advantages. People will stay tuned in waiting for what they expect will be the "real" message. Another strategy, one which I'm sure you can guess by now, is to put the most important message first. This too has its advantages. You know your audience's attention will be fresh. You will not have lost them as they consider whatever you shared first. The problem with this is the chances of them remembering anything that gets said after this most important message is likely to be quite small.

If you have a message that is so important that it is likely to overshadow any other message you intend to give, I recommend that you give only this one message as you speak with the other person or with the group you are addressing. In such situations, there is no sense to try "save time" by sharing more than the one overwhelmingly important item on your list.

An experience that was once relayed to me may help illustrate this point. A former workmate of mine told me of an experience he had when his entire workgroup, approximately 25 individuals, were being let go at the same time. They had all been asked to attend a meeting on short notice, like the afternoon of the day the meeting notice was sent. No one knew what the meeting was about - right up to the moment three people walked in carrying boxes of company folders filled with documents.

According to my friend, most people in the room were oblivious to what was in these folders, but my friend knew. One can imagine how a sick feeling in the pit of one's stomach would immediately develop in such instances. In fact, in that case, my friend said he got so immediately queasy that he had to leave the room. He knew what was going to be said and he had no interest in hearing it. While the people who brought in the boxes were not looking, he grabbed one of the portfolios and walked out. He went to his office grabbed his coat, walked out of the building, got into his car, and left.

And who would blame him? Is there any reason to sit in a room for even five minutes when the core message "We're letting you go?" Some companies will do what they can to lessen the drama. But honestly, in these situations how much of this information is going to actually be heard and remembered at that time? When heads are spinning with the reality of needing to meet next month's mortgage, no paycheck coming after two weeks, and, perhaps for some, zero money in the bank – details can be a bit difficult to take in. Best strategy, keep that type of meeting super short, end with "Information that will help is in your folders. We're here to answer what questions we can."

But this is an extreme case. Fortunately, most of us are not HR representatives who may someday need to deliver bad news like this to whole groups. More commonly, we are people who have important information to share but not so important as to impact one's immediate life or livelihood. In those extreme instances, you will definitely have their attention anyway, at least for few moments so regardless of how the message gets said it will be remembered.

How many times have you heard somebody say it wasn't so much the information that was shared, it was *how* the message was shared that bothered them? I bring up message preparation as the first of this three-part process because the *how* usually matters. If the information important enough that others need to hear it, understand it, and remember it, then it is important enough to put some time into the preparation of the message. So, by way of review, there are three steps in preparing the message. Identify the important components, create the most concise way to share this information, and determine the best order for delivering your points given the situation and the person or people you will be speaking to. Follow these steps and you will increase your chances of delivering messages that will be understood and remembered.

Preparing the Time and Place

After preparing the message, the next area to consider is preparation of time and place. I have already made reference to this next part of the process in the previous section. Consideration of time and place is important because if there is a disconnect between the message and the circumstances in which the message is shared, more weight might get put on the situation and less on the words. Tell me in the break room, for example, that I may need to work late, and I'm likely to laugh and say, "Thanks but no." When you say, "I'm not asking," I'll reply, "Oh, you're serious?"

In work situations, if you are a supervisor, you can easily arrange the appropriate time and place for any message you want to share. Usually, you would have an office and you can ask for a team member's time. Arranging an appropriate time and place requires a bit of extra effort. That's all.

In home situations, schedules can be very scattered. Finding time to sit down with a significant other can be quite the challenge. Still, if what needs to be said is as important, then working to find a time where the message can be shared without distraction and in a most appropriate matter is worth the effort. In the couples counseling world, it is not uncommon to hear the suggestion of a regular, weekly sit down to talk about whatever each person is thinking about. I'm not sure how many couples do this, but it seems like a good idea, right? It also seems that such times would be good for sharing important information with each other.

Children too can be hard to pin down, particularly in their teenage years. Early in my parenting life I received a great piece of advice. Arrange a time at least once a month to spend scheduled, one-on-one time with each child. I found the low-cost option of ice cream at our local fast-food place to be enticement enough to make this happen regularly. The practice created the type of relationship that when challenging things had to be discussed, the time and place for this was known and the connection was healthy enough to endure even through difficult conversations.

To sum up this section, the most important idea to keep in mind is that important messages require that time be set aside to show the importance of the message. Trying to say that something is important when no particular time or place has been set aside to discuss it doesn't compute. If the message is truly important, take steps to convey this. It may not be fun, comfortable, or easy, but it will be worth it.

Preparing the Person or People

Many of the ideas I will share in this section I have already alluded to or directly discussed in the previous chapter. The essential idea is this; when we have something important that needs to be heard, understood, and remembered, we need to ensure that we have done all we can to convey the importance of this message to the person or people we want to share it with. The entire previous chapter was an exercise in considering some of the possible ways that a person might not be prepared to hear, or is hampered in hearing, what we wish to say. Once these distractions are identified, we can then look for ways to minimize the potential impacts of these barriers.

A common home-based event is a person sitting on the couch watching TV while the other person attempts to share a message. In these cases, if you are the one who wants to share a message, the reality is the person who is focused on the TV, or the computer, or their game of Candy Crush, is not in a state to hear, to really hear, whatever it is you want to share. This is true no matter how much you might like it to be otherwise. In these situations, it is important to do what you can to prepare people to take in what you want them to hear. If they are not ready to listen, not just hear the words physically, but truly pay attention as you speak, then it it's simply not going to happen.

My next words of advice may seem like overkill. I say this from personal experience. In my home, whenever somebody has wanted to ensure I am paying full attention to whatever it is they have to say, they have typically turned off everything in the room – computers, televisions, cell phones, etc. They have kicked everyone else out of the room (goodbye kids, goodbye friends) and they've made sure that even the dog won't disturb us (sorry Fido). Then, with the room abnormally quiet, I am left with only one individual to focus on.

In my early years this would've been one of my parents. In my later years, it has been one of my children or my wonderful spouse. In most instances, even to this day I can tell you what most of those conversations have been about. This tells me something about how valuable it can be when we take steps to ensure we have a person ready to listen, really listen, to our message.

Now that the message planning and the conversation situation has been taken care of, the final step is the delivery. The magic words to begin with when it's time to share a message that you definitely want heard are these:

"What I am about to share is very important to me. For this reason, I am hoping it will be important to you too. Can you work with me on this?"

Obviously, nobody's going to hold you to using these exact words. You know the way that you typically talk. You know the person or people that you will be speaking to. Whatever you say, it has to come from the normal, natural, you. In other words, it has to be genuine. If the words you are thinking about opening with don't sound like you, rather than focusing on the words you've just said, rather than hearing, "Okay, I'm listening," you're more likely to hear, "Who are you?" This is not going to help your efforts.

So again, use the attention-getting words that are most natural for you; the statement that will express a sincere desire to be heard. The purpose of your attention-getting, attention-checking sentence is to ensure that the person or people you are speaking with understand that this is not just an everyday message, but in fact quite the opposite - that it is very important to you and because it is important to you, you need it be important to them. Starting any conversation with words like these should get the attention you're wanting. Words like these help you stop pretending you're being heard and actually get heard. Now let's look at work situations.

In the work world, in my work as a supervisor in many different organizations, I have found that having a one-on-one conversation at a time other than a regularly scheduled weekly occurrence tends to suggest that the topic being discussed needs particular attention. Similar to what I recommended for home and social situations, I have started these important conversations with a similar, very succinct statement. Something like this:

"What I am about to share is very important to me, and for this reason, it needs to be important to you too. Can you work with me on this?"

Sound familiar?

Similar words make sense to me because regardless of setting, when most people hear, 'The next words you hear are important to me, so I'm needing them to be important to you," they take note. Use a phrase that seems most natural to you but whatever words you use, be direct.

Again, you know yourself better than I do. You know the people you work with better than I do. So use the words that make the most sense for you. Just be sure that you are conveying the notion that what you are about to share is important and for this reason, it needs to be treated as such. After this is understood, then and only then, will it be the right time to move to delivering the message.

Now back to my experiences in supervising and passing along a reality check. Sometimes, no matter what we do, our message may not get heard, or if the message is heard, it may not get accepted. This is so because there are none so deaf as those who refuse to hear.

In this section I'm doing my best to share a method that will ensure that we have done all we can to communicate in a way that is most likely to be heard, understood correctly, and remembered. Unfortunately, what I cannot guarantee is what will happen after your message is delivered. The reason I cannot guarantee this is because in any communication transaction there are at least two people involved. And though the originator of the message (you) may be doing everything you can to be heard, understood, and remembered. Unfortunately, success in this arena lies also in the hands of the person or people at the other end of this exchange. End of disclaimer.

Case in point and back to our earlier recommendation, In work situations, what has surprised me on a few occasions over the 25 years or so that I've been supervising people is that even with a 'perfect' attention-getting, attention-checking, starting phrase and an outside-the-norm meeting time, I have still had team members who dismissed my messages as "not that important" or "just a passing thing." Not that the individuals in these cases used such words directly with me, but their actions after the conversation demonstrated they did not consider my message all that critical. Subsequent actions on my part made it very clear that I meant what I had told them. Yes, it required formal forms they needed to sign and representatives from human resource offices to be on hand to convey the same message, but we do what needs done.

If using reinforcement strategies and bringing in other individuals to repeat a message is needed to ensure that it is completely understood (even if not fully agreed with) than so be it. There is so much to say on this specific area of workplace communication that I dedicated an entire book to the topic. If you have a need in this area, get your hands on my boo, Change or Go: How to Stop Non Team Player Behavior at Work.

We're getting close to the end of the chapter now and there is no way I am going to end this chapter on a down note. Indeed, I think right here is where the core message of this entire book must rest; that if we adequately prepare our message, prepare the time and place, and prepare the person for what needs to be said then we will have done all we can to ensure the best delivery of our message. The title of this book was not selected by accident. Be aware, that despite our best efforts, there are times when we *think* we are being heard when we are not.

However, as we leverage preparation strategies, in-the-moment-strategies, and conversation follow-up strategies (the latter two coming in the next two chapters) we greatly increase our chances of truly being heard, understood, and remembered. I can't guarantee you success in every instance, but I can share with you what you can do to put the odds most assuredly in your favor for better success in this area that is so important for success at work, at home, and in our social endeavors.

Now let's take a look at strategies to increase the chances that your messages are understood in the way we intend them to be understood. This will be the topic of Chapter 4. In Chapter 5, I'll share with you several strategies to improve the chances that your message is remembered.

Chapter 4 - Setting the Hook

I'm not wild about the title of this chapter. I don't know what it is about my thoughts as I am writing this work. It seems I'm using my outdoor life experiences, particularly those of my youth - shooting, fishing, etc., to help me explain points in this book. Maybe I'm having a subliminal premonition that the bulk of those who read this work will be big time outdoor fans. I don't know. If you're not a big time outdoor fan, then please indulge me another outdoor experience of my youth.

As a child, I would go fishing quite regularly. My grandpa would take my older brother and me saltwater fishing. We would spend hours either on a boat or at the end of a jetty on the northern Oregon coast casting baited hooks into the ocean and then wait to see what would happen next. Usually nothing would happen, but every once in a while something would. One summer day while sitting on the jetty that pushed out into the Pacific I watched as others fishing off the same jetty were pulling in one fish after another – and good sized ones too! They seemed to be having a lot of fun. I wasn't. Grandpa watched for a while and then explained what he saw happening.

He said, "You've got fish eating on your hook just like everyone else does. Watch! See how your rod is being pulled down at the end there? That means you are doing a wonderful job of feeding fish down there who are smart enough to know that they're eating from a hook but that they are being careful as they do it. When you see this, if you pull back quickly on your fishing pole here, you'll hook one as he's eating. You'll catch a fish.

Grandpa was very much a hands-on kind of guy so he happily showed me personally what he meant. We waited for a few moments and just like he said, the pole bent down towards the water. At that moment he quickly jerked the rod and the fight was on. About 10 minutes later, after the fish was out of the water and on the ground by our feet. I saw what he was talking about. The hook had set inside the fish's mouth. This is what had caught the fish - something that would not have happened if we would have left the line as it was. Only after pulling back fast on the line was the hook able to do what it was meant to do.

Please, if you are not the outdoor type, if you don't like to fish, or if the idea of having a hook caught in the mouth of a fish makes you queasy or incensed, please think not on those thoughts. Instead, think more about the metaphor I am trying to share here.

Many times we will put an important message in front of people. Maybe they will hear it, maybe they won't. But even if they do hear it, we cannot be sure they understand it in the way we intend for it to be understood unless we take a few extra steps. This is what I mean by setting the hook.

In the first three chapters of this book, I took pains to share strategies that would help ensure you have the best situation possible for conveying a message to others. In this chapter I will give you several strategies to increase the chances that your message is not only heard, but that it is understood in the way that you intend your words to be understood. In the next chapter, I will share ideas for increasing the chances that your important message is remembered. I'm guessing you can see the logic behind these three steps. A message could be heard, but if it's not understood the way that we want it to be understood then we still have a problem. Similarly, even if a message is understood in the way we intended to be understood, if the message is not remembered, we still have a problem. My goal is to minimize your problems in this important area for both work life and home life; conveying a message, having it understood, and having it remembered.

First, I will share with you a strategy to *not* use. After you've shared your important message your next step is not to say something like, "Do you understand?" Of course, you can *say* this, many people do. But don't stop there. Why? Because in response to this question, most people will reply, yes, they understand. Unfortunately, this does not guarantee they understood your meaning in the way you intend for them to understand? What you know is that they *think* they understood. This is not the same thing.

Now of course, if the message is something more on the basic side, "Meet me in front of the store at 7 PM," you shouldn't need an elaborate confirmation strategy. One can be fairly certain that the message will be understood as intended. Complications arise when our messages are multi-faceted or they are coming from a very personal place.

This is one of the reasons why, in the previous chapter, I recommend you keep your important messages down to a relatively small number of important points for each important exchange. Give anyone a large list of items that they must understand and your chances of having them understand every point (let alone remember them) dramatically decreases.

To sum up, unless it's the most basic of messages, don't check understanding by simply asking, "Do you understand?" As I've already shared, this type of question is called a closed question because it generates only one of two possible answers, yes or no. And again, even if the person says yes, we can't know for sure that they understand our message in the way that we meant for it to be understood.

As we get into more effective strategies that can help confirm our message was understood as intended, I want to first preface the instruction with a bit of counsel. As you work to confirm understanding, be very careful not to sound self-righteous or condescending. Elementary teachers and parents will often go with the strategy of asking a young one to repeat back what they were told. That might work in those specific cases though even then I suspect the young one feels a bit patronized when being asked to do this. There is a 100% chance that an adult will most assuredly feel patronized to receive this treatment. So don't do it. As much as you might want to go with that very simple, easy to remember, and most natural strategy, don't do it. The likelihood of damage to the relationship is not worth it. The exception to this would be life-threatening, act-now-or-die type situations. In other words, extreme cases when immediate clarity is required and everyone involved would agree, urgency trumps all.

For the bulk of the situations you will encounter, here are some more productive comprehension check strategies. Use whichever one makes sense to you given what's most comfortable for you in the situation. It should go without saying not to limit yourself to just one strategy. For checking understanding, the more pathways you have, the better.

Discuss

This is one of those moments where what I write is going to seem like such common sense that you're going to think, "Duh!". My apologies, but in this case we really should start with the most obvious. Unfortunately, for many people, the most obvious way for checking understanding and hashing out the details is, or can be, the most difficult.

Some conversations, especially difficult conversations, are not easy to work through. (No doubt this is why they call them difficult.) Still, the improved result is usually worth the effort. For evidence of this I go back to my standard question that I ask of audiences I address. "What are the chances of change if there's no conversation about what needs to change?" Everyone knows the answer. There is, for the most part, a zero percent chance that anything is going to change if we don't have conversations about the change we're looking for. Hoping something might change is easy, but not at all effective. The only other option left is removing ourselves from the situation. I call this my three door philosophy.

But we're not here to talk about these three doors. We're here to talk about the one door that matters most this time and that is having a meaningful conversation around the topic that is important to you. Important that the conversation be had, important that the message be understood, and important that the message gets remembered. So consider this the moment where we walk over to the door and close it from the inside so that we do what needs done to convey the message we want to convey.

After sharing your concise message, it will be time to hear how it was received. Here are some example questions that can be asked to help facilitate discussion to check for understanding.

What do you think about this?
How do you feel about this?
Is there a different way you might have said this?
What are some ways we can work through this?
Where do you stand on this?
Tell me what strikes you the most about this.
If there were one or two parts about this you'd like to focus on, what would they be?

Given what I've said, what do you think is most important?
If you have to draw a picture of what I just said, what would
the picture include?

A variation on this strategy is to ask questions that connect
with priorities.

I'd like to hear your ideas. But first, what do you think about
what I've said? What should be tended to first, then second?
Can you see why this is important?
Do you feel it is fair, that I would like this to be important to
you too?
Are there parts of this that you have questions about?
What is most important to you about all of this?

As was said earlier, in your checking for understanding, be
sure you do this in respectful ways. Even with your efforts
along these lines, your listener may take offense, but it won't
be because you were offensive. It will be their interpretation
of the situation. We do what we can to create positive
interactions that foster communication but in the end, if the
other person translates the situation in less positive ways,
we do what we can to lessen the impact this, and move on.
How others react to our messages is something I will
address later in this chapter.

Look for Clues

This is not a category of possible statements to say or questions to ask, but rather what to look for. Body language can tell a lot. What is the person's expression? What direction are their eyes looking? What are they doing with their hands, their arms, their fingers? Are they sitting back relaxed and comfortable with arms open and legs comfortably apart? Or do you see somebody whose arms are held tight to their chest or maybe have their hands clenched?

Each one of these gestures and postures tends to carry some specific meanings. As I'm sure you already know, sitting back, with arms open and legs comfortably apart typically means the message is being well received. Or, at the very least, the individual is doing their best to maintain a neutral state as they hear what it is you have to say. On the other hand, eyes looking elsewhere and limited verbal responses usually suggest discomfort with what is being heard. It doesn't have to mean this. It could mean they are just soaking in and pondering the message. Asking exploratory questions such as those listed in the previous section should help to determine how your listener is feeling.

I think it's common knowledge that closed, and in particular clenched hands or arms folded and held close to the body are signs of a person who is not comfortable hearing what they are hearing. Your intent will never be to make someone uncomfortable. Your objective is simply to share information and ensure that your message was understood as intended. Though the information may not be comfortable to hear, if we consider the message only as information the heavy nature of a more challenging topic can sometimes be lightened. It's just information. And, whatever the message, most people would rather know than not know. Right?

I don't mean to suggest that as you check for understanding that you need to be a counselor too. In fact, I would lean towards suggesting that you *not* try to be the counselor if the information is, for any reason, not easy to hear. Let others process information in the way they feel they need to. Your job, your first priority, is to ensure that you have shared what you need to share and that they correctly understand it. In the next chapter we will talk about helping others remember the message. For now I just want to make sure that you have strategies in hand to help make sure that you and those you are speaking with are on the same page.

Responding to Responses

Depending on your message, the person you are speaking to, the complexity of the topic, and any number of other variables, there's likely to be a fair amount discussion after you have shared what it is you need to share. This may be particularly true if you followed the steps I outlined earlier such as setting aside a specific time for the conversation, clearing the room, and shutting off all distractions beforehand.

When questions come back your way, or when responses are a bit convoluted or multidirectional it's good to have some strategies ready to respond with. Asking clarifying questions is usually a good first strategy to go with. You want to make sure they have understood the message you wish to convey *in the way you mean for it to be understood.* Asking clarifying questions is usually a good first step towards achieving this goal. Here are some examples of clarifying or probing questions that can be asked.

Can you be more specific?
What makes you say that?
Can you share some examples?
Can you clarify that some more for me please?
Are you saying that…
Are you claiming…
Do you mean…

Handling Self Defense Mechanisms, or, In Other Words, Staying on Point

If you have the unfortunate situation of needing to share

information that will not be comfortable for the other person to hear, you need to be ready for the distinct possibility that the one you are speaking with is going to respond with words that take the focus off of the topic. This may be happening subconsciously, or quite consciously. Either way, the approaches they may take will be similar. I doubt I'm the first to notice this but in my experience those who are trying to take attention away from themselves and behaviors aren't what they should be will leverage one of three strategies. These strategies are defend, deflect, and deny.

As I discuss each one of these, I'm guessing you will recall past encounters where you have witnessed one of these behaviors coming at you. You may not have realized there was a pattern that people may fall into when faced with information they don't like or don't want to hear. Now you know. Knowing the possible reactions that can come your way can help you be prepared. Things may not go this way, but in case they do, let's take a closer look at each one of these self-defense strategies and discuss what to do when each one presents itself.

Defend

Here are a few examples of a defense response.

That's just who I am.
I can't help it if others don't like it.

If you or anyone else has a problem with this, it's their problem not mine.

I've always been this way. Why is this a problem now?

Reactions like these typically happen in work scenarios where a subordinate has been told that something in their behavior needs to change and, understandably, they are puzzled with the notion that what used to be okay may not be okay anymore. The fact is, what they had been doing probably was not okay, but there had been, up until that point, no manager who had sufficient nerve and/or professionalism to bring this to the attention of the employee and require that the behavior change.

On the home front, these same responses might be heard after sharing that something about the relationship needs to change. Again, understandably, a person who is faced with this information will naturally wonder why the issue is even being raised. They haven't changed. If it was okay before why is not okay now? And again, the reality is, it probably wasn't okay before. The difference is that you have decided that it can no longer go on as it was. At least not without saying something in an effort to work towards a more acceptable situation.

The best strategy for dealing with defense statements is to agree with them. It's true they have not changed. Then continue, with something similar to, "What *has* changed is it is no longer okay to have things go on as they have. Immediate responses to your message may be swift and not very kind. Nobody likes to hear that they need to change. Hearing this, many people will take the position that *they* should not have to change at all, so expect this.

If you are the supervisor in a work situation when this stance is taken, you have some very specific steps you can take. The short version of the rest of this scenario is yes they do have to change and you will work with them through whatever process the organization has in place to guide this change. If, after working the organization's steps, the change that is needed doesn't happen, it will be time for them to work elsewhere. At the risk of being self-promoting, I've written a book on this exact situation; cases where it's time to help somebody change or go. Indeed, this is the name of the book, *Change or Go*.

In personal situations; relations involving family, friends, or those you may work with in community groups, we do not usually get the advantage of enforcing our message so authoritatively. Actually, personal situations are more the opposite condition; if we want to maintain the relationship, we will need to do everything we can to help them see that yes, they may be who they are, but now at least one element of their behavior is becoming too difficult to be around and needs to change, or, at the very least, needs discussed to keep the relationship healthy. Hopefully you will be conversing with somebody who cares enough about the relationship to at least hear you out.

Deflect

I don't see you talking to anyone else about this.
I'm not the only one at fault here.
What's the big deal?
Really? This is the most important thing you think we need to discuss?

Deflection strategies are the equivalent of a verbal smokescreen. Actually all three of these strategies can be seen as smokescreens. But if we had to call out just one of the three for having particularly good diversionary properties, this would be the one. It's smoke and mirrors time! Individuals who respond with this strategy wisely get that owning the behavior won't get them anywhere and denying the behavior is futile so best to try and divert your attention to something else.

Because this is the most challenging of the three reactions to work with, I will use a separate section to provide a number of strategies for helping you stay focused on your topic. The strategies I will suggest will work with all three response types, but they are particularly helpful when working with deflectors. Here, I mean only to point out this is one of the self-defense strategies that you might encounter so that you know it when you see it.

Deny

Of the three self-defense strategies this is the most basic. This makes it the easiest to deal with yet at the same time potentially the most challenging reactions to work with. I'll explain. If the behavior is something that can be filmed, recorded, or found in the individual's work records then it's easy enough to show the individual what we are talking about and the defense that the behavior doesn't exist is overcome.

On the home front, the more common approach is to bring in two or three others to attest to whatever it is that's being denied. *"Yes darling, you do tend to respond in over critical ways when somebody is trying to help with the lawn."* Have three people in the house nodding their heads as this is being said and it is rather difficult to argue that it's just one person's perception of the situation.

On the other side of the spectrum, this can be one of the most challenging reactions to work with because those who deny a problem exists are not likely to do anything in response to the suggestion that there is a problem. The famed British clergyman of the 1600s, Matthew Henry, put it this way. "None so deaf as those who refuse to hear. None so blind as those who refuse to see."

As many recovery programs will affirm, awareness is the first step to recovery. If the one you are working with cannot see that there is a problem, even after discussing it, then you have a problem that's bigger than the topic itself. If this is a situation you have, then I'll remind you of the three door policy that was discussed earlier. We can hope for change, work to make change as best as possible, or remove ourselves (or the other person) from the situation. If you find yourself in the situation of working with an individual who holds firm in denial of something in a work situation, it will likely need to be door number three *for them*.

Maintain Control

Sharing a message that has the potential of generating upset feelings in another has the possible consequence of generating frustration or irritation in ourselves as well. This is natural. It is natural to want to fight fire with fire. And yet, to have any shot at a most productive result, we have to behave in a way that is contrary to our natural inclinations. We have to stay calm. Easier said than done? Yes, perhaps, but a necessity nonetheless.

Here are a few of the best strategies I can recommend for maintaining control:

<u>Take nothing personally</u>. Whatever insults, whatever actions, whatever words of denial, deflection, or defense come your way, accept that it would come out regardless of who was presenting the message to the one you are speaking to. These reactions are not personal, they are natural. And again, they would happen regardless of who was broaching the topic.

<u>Focus on your message</u>. Insults, defensive statements, deflective statements, and statements of denial all have one thing in common. They are meant to take you off topic. Don't let this happen. Listen to what is being said. Be polite, maintain composure, and keep bringing the conversation back to your core message. Here are a few examples to consider.

A: This has never been a problem before.
B: it's true the issue has not been raised before, but that does not mean it wasn't a problem. It's time to address it.

A: Why are you talking to me about this? Other people are doing it too.
B: Other people will be spoken with as needed. At this time, the conversation is between you and me.

A: What's the big deal? You need to grow a thicker skin.
B: Believe me, I am working on that. I'm asking for your help to meet me halfway.

Take a Time Out. If you find that the previous two strategies are not getting you anywhere. And you find your own temperature starting to rise, don't be afraid to take a time out. Nothing productive has ever been accomplished in anger and nothing ever will be. If you're going to have any chance of being successful both professionally and personally it is extremely important that you maintain your composure during these moments of heightened emotion. If it's necessary to pull yourself out of the conversation because your own emotions are going the wrong direction then so be it. Yes you started the interaction and it would be great if you could see it all the way through to a positive conclusion but when it becomes clear that a positive result is not going to happen during this first interaction, then see this for what it is and step away.

A key goal through all of this is to make sure that you do what you can to maintain a positive, productive relationship. If it is necessary to step away from the exchange in order to meet this goal, then that's what you do. There is no shame in this. In fact it really is the smarter move and anyone who would hear of your choice to disengage would agree.

Touching on this, there is a concept worth bringing up on this point. It's known as emotional intelligence. A summary version of the concept is the ability to recognize one's own emotions, control them if needed and use them as necessary to guide behavior. In layman's terms, and in connection to ourselves, emotional intelligence is being mindful of our thoughts and emotions and then changing strategies *as needed in the moment* in an effort to stay in control of a situation to achieve a desired outcome. Still not the most basic of language but I think you get the idea. The main point is this, regardless of whether you are at work, home, or in another social situation, if the interaction is not going well then stop the exchange and seek to take it up again at another time. As was said already, nothing good was ever accomplished in anger.

After closing an initially unproductive conversation, here are a few ideas to help you regain your own composure and move forward in a more productive manner.

- *Find a quiet place and breath. Take long, slow deep breathing, in through the nose, out through the mouth….and again, and again (You get the idea.)*
- *Take a walk. Enjoy the solace of the moment.*
- *Step into the restroom and put cold water on your face. Do not tear the towel dispenser off of the wall.*
- Go to the gym.
- Get your hands on a squeeze ball or a grip exerciser
- Pet a stuffed cat. Punch a plushy (in the privacy of your own work space of course).

Whatever it takes to release your frustration in a controlled manner, that's what you do.

When it's time to continue, you may find that the one you are speaking with will not want to meet again. Don't be too surprised about this. Avoidance is another strategy people can use to sidestep topics they don't want to discuss. Sometimes this happens for very logical reasons. For example, Harvey Mackay in his book *Swim with the Sharks without being Eaten Alive*, shared the experience of a local church group who refused to enter into "negotiations" that city officials had asked for. The church desired to obtain a permit for a neighborhood revival that they had held annually for many years. Some of the people in the neighborhood had tired of the prolonged volume-increased tradition and petitioned the city not to grant the permit.

The city, trying to find a happy medium, asked the church group to meet to discuss the issue. The church group, realizing the negotiation had the express purpose of changing their group, was not interested in entering into a negotiation. Their reply to the city was something like this. "We have asked for a permit to do what we have done for a number of years. It is your job to grant us this permit as you always have, or find cause not to grant the permit. We desire to stay constant in our worship. We pray that you too will remain constant in allowing us this."

I would hope that whoever you are working with will not be quite so steadfast in their ways but I can sympathize with individuals who feel they are being led into a situation where the desired outcome is for them to change. Always be open to options. Always look for alternatives. Express this. If a first conversation does not go well at first, express your desire for a best outcome for everyone and close the conversation by asking for a time the conversation can be picked up again. When the conversation continues, ask for their help in looking for resolutions and go from there.

Your next discussion could be a couple days later, perhaps four days, maybe even a week away. I would recommend not putting off your follow up discussion any longer than a week. In my experience, the chances that there will be a follow-up conversation go down after more than a week has passed so don't let this happen. If the topic was important enough to have in the first place, a few days delay should not make the topic any less important.

Chapter 5 - Helping People Remember

As I look back at the previous chapter, some may feel that getting into communication strategies for overcoming difficult conversations may seem a bit off-topic. Clearly, I think what some may consider a detour is worth the while. I believe this because any conversation that is uncomfortable is a conversation that tends to be remembered. We do not do ourselves any favors if we decide that the conversation is too difficult to have.

This is why I shared strategies to help you through more challenging conversations; to help you stay focused on the goal which is to ensure your message is heard, understood and remembered. As I'm sure you can infer from the title of this chapter, we're now going to get into making your message memorable.

There are a number of strategies that can be used at work to help people remember our messages. The standard strategies include follow-up meetings, follow-up email messages, posters on walls, conversations in the break room, in the halls, before or after meetings. These and many other activities can be called upon to help keep the message in the forefront of the minds of those we work with.

One of the most challenging work situations I know of is helping an organization change an aspect of its culture. Examples of this would be a factory that needs to refocus on safety after too many accidents have occurred, or a company whose employees need to truly believe that it is okay to make jokes, even 'harmless' ones at the expense of a minority worker. Culture is difficult to change because of its pervasive nature. Indeed, this is what makes it part of an organization's culture – it's everywhere.

Given this, if leaders want to see a change in an attitude or in actions that are 'everywhere' how is this done? It's done by putting the new message everywhere as well. All of the actions that were listed a few paragraphs earlier must be employed. A short list of strategies to employ could include email messages, signs in the halls and in the breakrooms, talking points when leaders meet with workers, agenda items for managers in meetings. An important point to keep in mind here is a one-time shot is not going to do it. Changing cultures comes from changing people. Knowing how difficult it is to change people, one quickly realizes the even greater challenge to changing the culture of an entire organization. It is doable but it MUST be something that is planned for over the long haul. No short-term strategy will 'stick'. Synergy for a previous way of thinking is strong. Organizational memories are short. The only way a message is going to be remembered by a larger group is if everyone receives that same message in multiple ways over an extended period of time. If this does not happen, chances are quite high that a culture will revert back to its earlier version after a message campaign has stopped

Workplace situations have the added advantage of financial incentive for remembering conversations. Indeed, if an employee too often forgets what they were told, it may well be that they won't have that job for very long, right?

Home scenarios are a bit different. Depending on the amount of technology used in the home, it's possible email can be used as a follow-up to conversations. It may seem a bit weird to email a spouse in the middle of the day to remind them about a dinner at the neighbors, but weird does not necessarily mean it shouldn't be done. Sometimes the more out of the norm an action is, the more likely the action is to be remembered. As we get more into this, think about the suggestions here, of course, but also ask yourself, "What are other strategies that might be good for where I work?"

I suspect our home is no different from other homes nowadays in that everyone in the home is carrying a cell phone. Texting messages to one another is also a great way to help people remember something that has been discussed. Another step down the technology trail is to add events to mutually-shared calendars. This is typical in the work world, it may not be a bad idea to use on the home front as well.

Have you ever experienced a singing telegram? If you have, you likely remember what the person was wearing, the tune they sang, and at least some of the words they sang as they stood outside your door and performed. Few would debate the memory enhancing behaviors of the singing telegram profession, so why not leverage at least a few of the same strategies when helping somebody remember a key message at home? Put your message to music.

If you're not a musical person, try wearing something you don't ordinarily wear - perhaps an ugly Christmas sweater or a particularly irreverent t-shirt. Be too distracting, however, and the attention will go to the distraction and not to your words. Think of a commercial you've seen or heard about which you can recall everything but the product that was being advertised. This is an example of what I'm talking about. It is *not* what you want to happen to your message. The lesson is to find the balance. Be creative with props but not so much so that others remember the moment but forget the message.

Many homes use a wall calendar. If the important message you have spoken with somebody about has to do with an event on an upcoming day then write that event on the calendar. Note it using large red letters if that will help. It also wouldn't be a bad idea to create flyers or construction paper signs to pin up on doors and walls and mirrors to also help people remember a key event on the family schedule.

In planning for family photos some time ago my good wife leveraged this particular strategy. We have five children most of whom, at the time, were in high school, running ten different directions. Bringing us all together for any length of time back then was a small miracle. Wanting to assure that every one of us would be in attendance for the photo session my wife made signs that went everywhere in the house.

She also added the event to every one of our cell phone schedules and wrote it in big red letters on the family calendar. In short, had anyone forgotten the event, there would have been no excuse. Fortunately, we have the type of family that actually likes to hang around each other and so getting everyone there was only a matter helping everyone remember the date. With an appreciative nod to my family, convincing them they had to be there wasn't an issue.

Creating pictures can also be a useful strategy for helping people remember a message. There is a reason why the making of movie posters is a form of art unto itself. Put an image in somebody's mind and that image is likely to stay in one's thoughts for quite some time. You want a child to remember something you discussed? Have them draw a picture about it. If you're fortunate enough to be working with adults who still have a bit of child in them, consider the same strategy. Bring out the box of crayons you might have laying around and some plain white sheets of paper and go nuts!

Understand that when it comes to helping somebody remember a message that you want remembered nothing should be considered too outlandish. Yes, it would be nice, it would be wonderful, it would be a fantastic thing, if all we had to do was say what needed to be said and have everything remembered. Wouldn't it be nice if the person we are speaking to internalized everything and recalled it as needed when needed? Sadly, most people aren't that good.

Think back to the first chapter of this book where two conversation examples were given. In both conversations people talking to Mark was asked a question that went something like this.

Don't you remember we talked about this?

If you find yourself asking something like this to a person you KNOW you spoke to earlier about a particular topic, do you need any more evidence that your message was not remembered? Probably not. If you're still hearing this after using the strategies discussed, it's time to pull out all of the stops and pile on even more strategies to get your message remembered.

Bonus Memory Strategy #1 Lean on Favorites

Does the receiver of your message like jerky? If so, hand him or her a small package of jerky with a note on it that reads, "Don't be a jerk" followed by the message you need them to remember.

Is the receiver of your message a sports fan? If the answer is yes, hand them an object of that sport with the important message taped to that object, (or maybe even written on it). I still have a tennis ball I was given years ago that has a specific date written on it. The date was my daughter's last high school tennis match. I didn't miss the event.

Most of us have about a thousand things going on in our lives. Accept this and realize that people may need help remembering messages. Not because they think what is important to you is not important to them but because their minds are more focused on the immediate. If your message doesn't involve an immediate concern, it's not going to be 'top of mind'. Don't take it personally, just adjust for it.

Does the person who needs to remember your message like to cook? If so, a recipe card might work.

<u>Recipe for an Awesome Friday Evening</u>

1. Make reservations at your favorite restaurant

2. Do not work late Friday night. Better yet, leave early.

3. Be ready to receive a special gift at dinner.

Is there any chance your partner will forget the plans for this coming Friday? Sadly, still yes, but hopefully not a big chance.

Bonus Memory Strategy #2 Leverage Others

If the message is not to personal, ask other people to help you out. Before going any further, I will give a disclaimer here. I KNOW this is likely to be annoying to the target of your message. But again, remember the goal here, we want the message to be remembered. If you can use this strategy, the one whose memory you are trying to help will be hard-pressed to say, they didn't remember.

If a friend needs help remembering to bring something to an event, call the friend's family to enlist their help reminding the friend.

If someone in the house needs help remembering to change the oil in the car, ask a coworker of theirs to tape a note to their workstation, work vehicle, or other often seen piece of work equipment.

By now, I'm hoping that you get the point of this final step. It would be nice if all we had to do is say something and the message got locked away in the memory of the one we are communicating with in such a way as to be recalled correctly whenever that information was needed. Unfortunately, that's simply not reality. Helping others remember what it is we've said will often require follow-up. The more creative that follow-up can be, the more likely the message will be remembered. Yes, it is unfortunate that we have to take these extra steps to facilitate most effective communication but if this in fact is our goal then we have to be willing to take these extra steps.

Think back on a conversation you may have had a long time ago. What was it about that conversation that helps you remember it even to this day. Whatever attributes that experience had, this may suggest to you what same elements will help you create a memorable message today for someone else.

Conclusion

In this book I have done my best to share with you what I believe is a winning strategy for ensuring the message is heard, understood, and perhaps most importantly remembered. I've leveraged years of work and home life experience to put together a number of ideas, strategies, and tools to help you be more effective in the conveyance of discrete item matters at both home and work environments.

I am fully aware that I have not given you every possible scenario for every possible situation to help you with this goal. Despite this shortcoming I sincerely hope that you find enough information in this book to help you be more effective in your home and work communication.

Perhaps I should have addressed this in the introduction. It's not as if there aren't already thousands of communication-related books on the market. What am I bringing to the table that isn't already out there?

This is a good question. The differences here is in providing an end-to-end strategy and in the way this information is presented. I think a key to conveying our most important messages is a three-step process that involves first being heard, second ensuring that we are understood, and then doing whatever we can think to do to be remembered.

Now let me tell you a little secret. These three steps are the steps I keep constantly in my mind as I deliver keynote presentations to organizations around the world. Sharing this knowledge is just the first step. If the information is heard but not understood, then it's useless. If the information is understood but not remembered, again, the information is useless. I have no interest in sharing information that doesn't get used. My guess is that you have no interest in sharing information in your own homes and workplaces that does not get used. And so I offer you these ideas.

It is my sincere hope that you will find value in the ideas I have shared here. Please know that I am always open to hear more about how to be even more effective in this important area of life, both home life and work life. I make no secrets about how to get in touch with me. If you feel there is something I can and should share in this arena that will be helpful in the lives of others that I speak to in the future, please don't hesitate to reach out and share your thoughts with me. I will be happy to hear them.

Dream big dreams, and make them happen!

About the Author

Arron Grow, is owner of AP Grow and Associates. He has over 25 years of experience in organizational and individual development. His experience includes many years overseeing for-profit operations on university campuses both state-side and overseas. In business and industry his service includes work as an international program manager for Microsoft as well as Organizational Development and Continuous Learning Manager on the West Coast for Green Mountain Coffee Roasters.

Keynote speaker Dr. AP Grow specializes in sharing most effective, misery-free management and team-building strategies. He adds value to organizations by guiding managers to be what every employee wants and what every organization needs.

Works by AP Grow

books, ebooks, and audiobooks available through amazon.com

Change or Go:
How to Stop Non Team Player Behavior at Work

How to Not Suck as a Manager

Stop Pretending You're Being Heard: What to do When the Message Really Matters

You Know You Want It, Here's How to Get It: Lessons Learned from My Years as Executive Producer of Personal Best Radio

Notes

STOP PRETENDING YOU'RE BEING HEARD

www.ingramcontent.com/pod-product-compliance
Lightning Source LLC
Chambersburg PA
CBHW060624210326
41520CB00010B/1461